eBay 30 Day Challenge

How to Make $1000 in your First 30 Days

Ready – Set – Sell

Copyright © 2014 by Braun Schweiger

Table of Contents

Table of Contents 3

Why You Need to Read This Book 5

About me 7

Why eBay 10

What Should I Sell? 14

Sourcing Items to Sell 17

    Yard Sales / Estate Sales / Auctions 18

    Retail stores – Wal-Mart Target T J Maxx 20

Posting Your First Listing to eBay 22

    1. Product Research 22

        Using the Advanced Search Tool 23

    2. Title 24

    3. Photos 25

    4. Description 27

    5. Price 30

    6. Shipping / follow up 32

Tips & Tricks to Increase Your Sales 36

eBay fees 41

Final Wrap up 43

Why You Need to Read This Book

Welcome to the *eBay 30 Day Challenge*. The goal of this book is to help you move from zero to $1000 in just 30 days by selling everyday items on eBay.

And, the great thing is—anybody can do it!

Selling on eBay doesn't require any special skills, education, or experience. All you need is access to a computer, a digital camera, and something to sell.

The way this book is laid out, I'm going to tell you a little bit about me—and how I got started selling on eBay. Then we'll talk about eBay, and why it's the best choice for anyone to make money—NOW!

After that, I'll drop a few hints about what sells best on eBay, and how to find these items around your house, at local garage and estate sales, or even at retail stores like Wal-Mart, SAMs, and Costco.

Finally, I'll share everything you need to know to post your first listings on eBay. After that, it's a simple matter of getting started. I'll show you how to post your items, sell—ship—repeat.

That's really all there is to it. Find an item to sell. Determine the best price, and method to list it on eBay. Wait for it to sell. Collect your money, and repeat the process.

About me

I've been selling on eBay for over ten years now.

My typical work week is forty to fifty hours, Monday through Saturday, and maybe another hour on Sunday checking everything and answering emails. Most weeks I make $1000 to $1200. Some weeks I make double that. It just depends on what items I have listed for sale that week.

My schedule goes something like this. I visit garage sales, estate sales, and auctions on Thursday, Friday, and Saturday. Saturday afternoon I clean everything up real good, and get it ready to photograph. Monday, Tuesday, and Wednesday I photograph and list my items.

I mail items daily Monday through Friday to meet eBay's Top Rated Seller requirements.

I've got the eBay app on my cell phone. It's set to send out notifications whenever I receive a question or sell something so I can run my business on the go. If I'm on the line about buying something—I check what it's selling for on eBay or Amazon, and make a buying decision based on real numbers—not some price I hope to get for it.

I know other sellers who hit the road for several weeks at a time like the American Pickers. They check out every estate sale and auction within a hundred miles, or five hundred miles. Most of the people who do this have a partner back home who does the actual listing, packaging, and shipping.

Several of the couples I know who do this are pulling down over $100,000 a year selling on eBay and Amazon. It's just a matter of scaling up once you get the process down.

Keep in mind—the premise behind this book is to get you started, familiarize you with the process, and to help you make your first thousand dollars.

After that, you'll have a good idea if selling on eBay is right for you. My recommendation is to take it slow. Make your first thousand dollars, sit back, and think about what you want from selling on eBay.

Do you want to make a few hundred dollars a month to help make ends meet? Do you need to pay off some bills, save up for a down payment on a new house? Or are you trying to replace your day job, and become a full time at home worker?

No matter which option you choose—it's all possible selling on eBay.

Success is just a matter of getting started.

Why eBay

If you're not familiar with eBay, the best way to think of it is like a ginormous garage sale or yard sale—only it's online.

Buyers and sellers meet on eBay to exchange items and services for cash. In its early days eBay was a perfect marketplace. Most items sold at auction. Whoever made the highest bid won the item. Today all of that has changed, and most items sell with a fixed price. When you see something you like, you click on it, and agree to buy the item at the set price.

At the end of 2013 eBay had nearly 149 million registered users, who spent over $78 billion dollars (exclusive of eBay Motors). Amazon came in just behind eBay with $74 billion dollars in sales, collected from over 243 million registered users. The only larger online marketplace is China's Alibaba and Alibaba Express.

The final fact to keep in mind is the online market place is going mobile. In 2013 just under 30 percent of online sales were completed using mobile devices such as an iPhone,

Smart Phone, or tablet. By the end of 2014 that number is expected to approach 50 percent.

The reason I mention this is to help you understand two key factors.

1. Online sales are going up, and
2. More sales are taking place on mobile devices, which means people are shopping on the go—when they're at work, at school, or visiting with friends.

To be successful selling on eBay, you need to keep these two trends in mind when you're buying, selling, and listing items. You need the right product, lots of pictures, and a short action filled description.

To make as many sales as possible you need to make it easy for customers to buy from you.

eBay has two different types of listings that will be used by most sellers.

- Auction listings are just like going to a local auction. Items are offered for sale, and the buyer who makes the highest bid wins. Until a few years ago most listings on eBay were sold at auction. Today most items sell at a fixed price.

eBay has a buy-it-now option sellers can add to auction listings. Buy-it-now gives bidders the option to pay a higher price and purchase the item right now, rather than waiting for the auction to close. The main thing to remember is: eBay requires the buy-it-now price to be at least 30 percent higher than the starting price.

Auctions can run for one, three, five, seven, or ten days. The standard auction is for seven days. eBay charges sellers an extra fee if they choose to run a ten day auction.

In most cases, a seven day auction will work just fine to bring the most money for your items. One, three, and five day auctions can be used when you have multiples of fast selling items. An example would be new or used iPhones. Most bidding takes place the last day of an auction so sellers can speed up the process by running shorter term listings.

If you have an expensive item, like a rare book or comic book, that is expected to draw lots of bidders, a ten day auction will attract the maximum number of bidders. As a result you should be able to get a higher price for your item.

- Fixed Price listings are just like going to your local department store. If you see an item you like, you place it in your shopping cart, and buy it at the shelf price. The majority of items sold on eBay today sell at a fixed price.

eBay has a best offer option sellers can use with fixed price listings. It lets buyers send sellers an offer to purchase their item at a discounted price. Buyers are allowed to make three offers, so you can dicker back and forth—and agree on a price that works for both of you.

You can set the length of a fixed price listing, but the two most popular choices are 30 days, and good until cancelled. I recommend the 30 day option because when your item ends you can revisit it to make any necessary changes to give it a better shot at selling the next time around

What Should I Sell?

What should I sell on eBay?

That's the million dollar question.

The truth is: just about anything will sell on eBay. It's just that some items take longer to sell than others. Examples of fast selling items are electronics, cell phones, name brand clothing, and new release movies and CD's.

A lot of sellers list old books, VHS tapes, sports cards, and other collectibles, but items like these take longer to sell. You have to wait for the right buyer to come along. Sometimes it can take a week; sometimes it can take a year. You've just got to price your items higher to cover the extra time period and listing fees.

eBay Best Sellers

As a general rule the following items are traditionally some of the hottest selling items on eBay.

- Cell phones
- Personal electronics
- Laptops
- Tablets
- Stamps
- Coins
- Rare books
- Name brand clothing
- Designer clothing
- Jewelry
- Watches
- Movies
- Auto Parts
- Non-working electronics (cell phones, tablets, laptops, Kindles)

Some items are a tough sell right now. Here are several items on the slow moving list.

- Damaged or broken items
- Beanie babies
- Newer toys (from the last ten or fifteen years)

- New books
- Dollar store items
- Sports cards (produced after 1980)

I recommend getting started by selling items you already have around the house. That way you can take eBay out for a free trial run and make sure it's right for you.

Not everyone is cut out for online selling.

Contrary to what most magazine articles and how-to books have to say, selling on eBay isn't all sitting around the house in your jammies or undies. There's some actual work involved.

Sourcing Items to Sell

One of the toughest things for new or existing sellers is deciding what to sell on eBay.

My suggestion is to start out selling items you already have around the house. Here's a quick list to get you started.

- Clothes
- DVDs & CDs
- Old electronics (laptops, Kindles, tablets, and cell phones)
- Video games
- Shoes
- Books
- Collectibles (Baseball cards, comic books, Hummel figurines)
- Old landline phones

The list goes on, but you get the idea. Just because you no longer use an item doesn't mean it doesn't have any value. Used clothing and electronics are huge sellers on eBay.

Just because your kids stopped playing their old video games doesn't mean someone else won't want them. The same goes for DVDs and CDs. You may be tired of watching and listening to them, but someone else out there is dying for the opportunity.

Not every item will sell. Not right away anyway, but don't be afraid to list them. It is good practice, and many of the items you put up for sale will sell.

It's like paid on the job training.

Yard Sales / Estate Sales / Auctions

The next step for most sellers is to pick up items at yard sales, estate sales, and auctions.

You read about all of these great finds where people pick up rare first edition books for $5.00, or snatch a rare print or painting for a few bucks; all I can say is don't get your hopes up quite that high.

I look for books and magazines I can pick up for a dollar or two and resell for ten or twenty dollars each. Clothes are a good find especially, name brand kids clothing like

Gymboree and Osh Kosh. Women's plus size clothing is a consistent seller. Name brand jeans sell well, as do any name brand outfits like Anne Taylor, Banana Republic, Tory Burch, Ralph Lauren, and J Crew.

Collectibles are a crap shoot. Keep your first few buys in the five and ten dollar range. After you get a feel for things raise your limit to twenty-five or fifty dollars. If you get the urge to buy something expensive, check the eBay app on your cell phone first to make sure of what it's selling for. I remember my first few estate sale buys. I picked up some liquor decanters I was sure I could triple my money on. I soon discovered they were selling for less than I paid for them.

Smaller auctions are another great place to pick up items to resell on eBay. I check the listings online or in the paper before I go to make sure they have items that interest me. When I get to the auction site I make a quick round of those items, and check the value on my eBay app. Before the bidding starts I set a limit on how much I'll bid. That way I don't get caught up in the moment and overspend.

Most estate sales run Thursday thru Saturday. Prices are higher the first two days, and are often times reduced by as much as fifty percent on the last day. I normally make two trips. I try to get there early the first day and pick up any items I really want then. I make a note of items I'd like to have and check back the last day of the sale to see if they still have the item, and how much it's selling for. Sometimes you lose the item by waiting, but you don't make anything if you overpay, so you've got to learn to balance time and money.

Retail stores – Wal-Mart Target T J Maxx

Sometimes the best deals are right under your nose.

Retail stores are constantly changing their inventory—culling out slow sellers, making room for next season's merchandise, or the next holiday. Many eBay sellers have discovered this is a great way to play the system and make a great profit.

Smart sellers hit the clearance aisles every day. Many of them scan bar codes or punch items into their cell phones to determine what the items are selling for on eBay.

Look for clothing that is being closed out at the end of the season. Often times you can find coats, swim suits, and other apparel being closed out for pennies on the dollar. Some sellers resell them immediately, but smart sellers pack the items away until the beginning of the season next year. Often times they can sell the items for full price.

Holiday items are another favorite buy for clearance sellers. You can get some great deals a few days after Christmas, Halloween, and Easter. Once again, you'll make the most money by holding the items until the next year.

I've picked up a lot of close out shoes at Shoe Carnival for ten and fifteen dollars and resold them for twenty-five dollars or more.

If you live in an area with a winning sports team, especially a local college bowl winner you may be able to make a profit purchasing items at full price.

Tools are always a quick sell, as are auto parts, hardware, and small appliances.

Best advice I can give you, if you're new to shopping clearance aisles for resale keep your purchases small. If you're looking at big dollar items check them against the eBay app first, or have someone home at the computer and have them look the item up for you.

The last thing you want to do is lose money.

Posting Your First Listing to eBay

There are six steps to creating a good product listing on eBay.

1. Product research
2. Title
3. Photos
4. Description
5. Price
6. Shipping / Follow up

1. Product Research

The first step to a successful listing is performing product research.

Most times good product research will give you the answers to the other five listing essentials.

To research an item you want to use eBay's advanced search feature. To access it move your cursor to the search box at the top of the eBay page. Just to the right of it you'll see the word *advanced*. Select it. This will take you to the advanced search tool.

The most important thing to remember is: only sold items count. There are a lot of items listed on eBay and Amazon with all sorts of crazy prices, but the only items that count are the ones somebody is willing to pay money for. If nobody laid down any cold hard cash for it, it's just somebody wishing to make a sale. The information in these listings won't help you become a better seller. The only reliable information you can find is in sold listings.

Using the Advanced Search Tool

To get started using the advanced search tool, enter three or four keywords into the search box. In the next section titled *search including* place a check mark by *sold listings*. There are a lot of other options to choose from but for now I would stick with these two, and possibly *buying formats* and *condition*.

The items returned in search will have the price listed in green, and there will be a green bar along the bottom of the listing picture with the word sold written in it.

The first thing you'll notice is the price each item sold for. When you click into an item you'll be able to examine it closer. Make a note of which keywords the seller included in the title, how they worded their description, which buying format they used to list the item, what the starting price was, and if a buy-it-now price was used, make a note of what it was.

Finally, take a look at the pictures. How many pictures did the seller include in their listings? What type of pictures were they—Close-up? Wide angle? Well lit? Were the pictures of just the item being sold, or did they include accessories, too?

2. Title

Think of the title as the entry point to your listing. It should contain all of the search words buyers will use to find your item.

Some sellers like to get cutesy with their titles or write complete sentences, but that's a waste of valuable real estate. eBay gives you 88 characters to describe your item. Make every one of them count. Here are a few items you should include: product name, maker / manufacturer, model number, color, size, condition, warranty, and any common misspellings.

Don't waste words saying awesome, cool, LQQk, or anything like that. No one searches on these terms. Also, resist the urge to capitalize everything. ALL CAPS make your title hard to read, and it makes you look desperate—it's sort of like you're begging for attention.

Final piece of advice: use every character available to you.

3. Photos

Other than your title, good photos are the key to making more sales. Many sellers don't even bother to include a description, they just post a half dozen or a dozen high resolution pictures and invite sellers to decide for themselves if it's the right item for them.

My thought is you want to include as many pictures as possible. Include views from as many different angles as you can. Make sure you snap a few pictures of the packaging and any accessories.

Shoot a quick video of the item you want to sell. It doesn't have to be anything elaborate. If you're selling clothes it could be someone wearing the outfit you're selling. If you're selling toys, show some kids playing with them.

People are fascinated with video. Many times they'll click on it just because it's there. Video is a great way to get extra eyes on your listings.

The first picture you post is the most important. It's the gallery picture for your listing, or the one buyer's will see along with your title in search.

It's the money shot.

You need to make your gallery picture sizzle. It can be a shot of the item and accessories, a close-up of any detail work, or a shot of the product in use. Keep in mind, you can't superimpose words over your gallery image, and it can't be a drawing. It's got to be a picture.

eBay has a few other rules and requirements for pictures. All pictures are required to be a minimum of 500 pixels along the longest side. eBay recommends 1600 pixels for the best viewing experience. The reason this is important is when buyers click on your images to blow them up, the larger your picture, the more detail they're going to be able to see.

Let's say you're selling a hand tooled leather saddle. You can talk forever about horses, cattle, and cowboys riding on the open plains, but one close up picture will close the deal quicker. When the buyer clicks on a picture they can zoom in section by section to really check out all of the detailed leather work. It's the next best thing to being there.

The same thing goes when an item you're selling is damaged. You can describe the damage, or you can show the damage and invite buyers to decide for themselves how bad it is.

Good pictures will help you make more sales. Good pictures will help to prevent returns and misunderstandings. Invest in a good camera, and take time out to learn how to use it. Your investment will pay off in increased sales.

4. Description

A good description should tell the buyer everything they need to know to make them want to buy your item. At the same time, it should be short, concise, and have plenty of white space.

Buyers read item descriptions the same way they read blog posts and other internet content. They scan your listings looking for details that interest them.

Make it easy for buyers to find the information they need to know. Give your item details in short bursts. Use a large headline followed by one or two short sentences. Use another headline, and include all of the specs or other pertinent details using a bulleted list.

Reader's eyes are naturally drawn to bold text, and we're used to finding the info we're looking for in bullet points, so our eyes go there next.

Here's an example of what you should shoot for.

1955 Topps Willie Mays Sports Card

If you're a fan of 1955 Topps baseball cards you know the Willie Mays card is one of the most desirable. Take it from me—this is one of the best examples of that card you'll find.

Item Details

- *1955 Topps Baseball card*
- *Card # 194*
- *4 solid corners*
- *Mint to near mint condition*
- *Perfectly centered back*
- *Lustrous vibrant color – just like the day it was printed*

Send this card in for grading and watch the value go up.

One other thing you will notice is I made a call to action at the end of the description—"Send this card in for grading and watch the value go up." Another effective call to action would be, "Grab this key Willie Mays card now before another collector outbids you."

A call to action doesn't always work, but it gives you one last shot at making the sale.

Keep it short, simple, and to the point.

Buyers don't want to waste time wading through a lot of clutter and unnecessary words. They want to find the information they want—NOW! Help them find it, and you will make more sales.

One other thing. Never—ever fill your descriptions with conditions, policies, disclaimers, and other gobbledygook. Nothing turns buyers off quicker than looking at this stuff.

Keep your descriptions positive. Don't tell buyers what you won't do. Tell them what you will do. Focus on helping customers buy from you. Don't warn them that they need to follow through with their bid, and that their bid's a valid legal contract and all that other nonsense. All of that stuff only does one thing—It tells potential buyers you're a prick, and they should move on to the next listing.

5. Price

Setting the price is part art, part science, and a whole lot of luck.

Some sellers swear by starting every auction at 99 cents and letting the market set the price. Other sellers shoot for the moon. They slap a crazy price on every item they sell, and add a best offer to see what buyers are thinking. Some sellers shoot to double or triple their initial investment and price everything accordingly.

There's no one set way to price your items.

My suggestion is to research everything. Before you list anything on eBay run an advanced search by sold items so you know what your item recently sold for. Most often, you'll discover it sold for a range of prices depending upon condition and how well the description was written.

If you're selling your item in an auction listing, set your starting price at the lowest price the item sold for, and then set a buy it now price just above the highest selling price. This virtually assures that your item will sell.

If you're selling your item in a fixed price listing set the selling price just above the highest price the item most recently sold for. Include a buy-it-now, and set it to automatically accept at the lowest recent selling price, or another price that is acceptable to you.

If you have an item that hasn't sold recently or is totally new to eBay you have a few choices.

If you have a suggested selling price in mind—list the item as fixed price, and add a best offer. This will help you see where the market is at.

Alternatively, you could start your item at 99 cents, $9.99, or some other price, and see where the market takes it.

After you've sold one or two items, you can use this pricing information to price your other listings.

6. Shipping / follow up

The first decision you have to make is whether to offer free shipping or charge for shipping.

eBay encourages sellers to offer free shipping, and usually ranks items with free shipping higher in search, so if your margins allow you to offer free shipping, do it.

If free shipping isn't an option for what you're selling, check what other sellers are charging for shipping on similar items. There are several different options for showing shipping charges. If you can, wrap part of the shipping fees into your item price, and charge less shipping than other sellers. If you can't do that, try to charge $1.00 less for shipping than your competitors.

eBay offers several different shipping options.

- **Flat rate**. Flat rate shipping means you charge the same shipping fees to all customers no matter where they are located. The advantage is buyers know exactly what they have to pay.

- **Calculated shipping**. Calculated shipping uses eBay's shipping calculator to determine shipping fees based upon where your buyer lives. The advantage is buyers who live closer to you get a break on shipping, which can reduce their total purchase price.

- **Freight**. Freight shipping is for larger items that need to ship by motor truck. The eBay shipping calculator only works up to 150 pounds, so if your item weighs more than that you need to use flat rate.

- **Local pickup**. Local pickup lets buyers pickup items at your home or business location. Be cautious if you accept payment through PayPal. With local pickup you don't have delivery confirmation if the buyer opens an item not received case against you.

Follow up

Check your email at least two or three times a day when you have items for sale.

The quicker you can respond to buyers the more likely you are to close the sale. When you respond to a customer be sure to answer their question completely. Also, take a few minutes to talk up the item you are selling. Say something like, "Thank you for inquiring about the widget I have for sale on eBay. It's a great widget, and in fantastic shape. You can read a little bit more about it in this blog post."

It only takes a few more minutes when you respond to your buyer, but it helps to build confidence in your eBay store and what you're selling.

If you receive a complaint after you sell an item, don't panic. Thank the customer for contacting you, and tell them you understand their concerns. Most often you can save the sale by taking a few moments to explain how to use the item, or by answering any other questions your buyer may have.

If the customer insists on returning your item, accept the return graciously, and outline your return policies. If the buyer is required to pay return shipping let them know, and tell them how soon they can expect a refund.

If the return is because of a defect in the item or a misstatement in the listing—apologize for the mistake. Offer a refund, or replacement if available, and once again explain the return process.

Handling inquiries and returns professionally will help ensure positive feedback from the transaction.

Tips & Tricks to Increase Your Sales

1. **Use eBay & PayPal shipping tools.** When you print your labels using the eBay shipping tool it automatically transfers buyer information into the shipping label saving you time. It also transfers tracking information back into the item listing page so buyers can track their items progress. The other advantage is you pay for shipping as you go. Each time you print a label the shipping price is deducted from your PayPal account.

2. **Get free shipping supplies from the USPS.** Stop paying for boxes, and packing supplies. The post office will give you free boxes and envelopes for items you ship by priority and express mail.

3. **Use GoDaddy Bookkeeping to track your income and expenses.** eBay has an app called GoDaddy Bookkeeping that can help you keep track of your earnings and expenses. The great thing is it can

automatically import information from eBay and PayPal, as well as from any credit cards and bank accounts you connect to the app. If you sell on Amazon or Etsy, GoDaddy Bookkeeping works with them, too. The cost is $9.99 per month.

4. **Add YouTube videos to your auction listings.** Videos can help engage auction viewers, and increase the likelihood they will buy from you. It's simple to add YouTube videos to your listing descriptions. Just upload your video to YouTube, and select use *old embed code*. Paste the code into your item description where you want the video to appear.

5. **Use Templates or Sell Similar item to streamline your listings.** When you use a template or the sell similar item option all of your listing information is transferred to the new listing. This saves you from typing repetitive information.

6. **Offer Shipping discounts.** When you offer shipping discounts, customers are likely to purchase additional items from you. eBay gives you several options to choose from. You can ship additional items for free, or at a reduced rate.

7. **Skip listing upgrades**. Whenever you list an item eBay offers several listing upgrades that are supposed to increase visibility for your item. Most of them are a waste of money. The only one that may help is subtitle. Depending upon the item you are selling, subtitle can give buyers the extra nudge they need to click into your auction and give it a look.

8. **Opt into eBay's Global Shipping Program**. eBay's Global Shipping program lets you sell internationally without all of the hassle of filling out customs forms and such. To get started you just need to select the Global Shipping Program option. If your item sells internationally, you ship it to eBay's shipping center in the United States and you're done.

9. **Only accept PayPal**. eBay gives sellers a number of payment options, but 99 percent of buyers use PayPal. Don't waste time fooling around with other payment providers.

10. **Always ship with a tracking number**. Ship all of your items with a tracking number. It keeps everyone involved in the transaction honest. Tracking allows

buyers to know where their package is any step along the way. If something goes wrong, it can protect you if an item not received case is filed. If you ship with eBay's shipping tool, tracking is automatically uploaded into the item listing.

11. **Include best offer in your fixed price listings**. Best offer lets sellers send you an offer for items you list by fixed price. Each time they send you an offer, you have the chance to accept it, or send a counter offer. Buyers are able to send three best offers on each item. Don't be afraid to bargain back and forth if the offer you receive is too low.

12. **Include buy-it-now in your auction listings**. Buy-it-now is an option where buyers can buy your auction listing for a set price, and end the auction immediately. In my experience, one in nine auctions will end with a buy-it-now. The only requirement is your buy-it-now price must be at least thirty percent higher than your starting price.

13. **Accept returns**. Most people are reluctant to buy an item sight unseen from a buyer they don't know. You can overcome this fear and sell more items by

offering to accept returns. In my experience, less than one in five hundred items is returned, so it shouldn't be a major concern.

14. **Schedule Pickups with the USPS.** Stop going to the post office. If you are shipping at least one item by priority or express mail you can schedule a pickup, and the post office will come to your house and pick up your packages.

15. **Open an eBay store.** If you sell a lot of items on eBay, an eBay store can help you ramp up sales even more. eBay stores allow you to collect all of your items in one spot on eBay. If you choose to, you can brand your store and listings so they are easily recognizable as your own. An eBay store also opens up several other features including being able to build an email list and send newsletters to your subscribers, and to use Mark Down Manager—an eBay tool that lets you discount items in your store for a short period of time.

eBay fees

On eBay sellers have to pay to play. eBay charges a myriad of fees. These include listing fees, final value fees, upgrade fees, and store fees (if you have a store).

The following list is included to give you an idea of eBay fees. It is up to date as of August 25th, 2014.

Seller fees are based upon whether you have an eBay store or not, and the level of eBay store you have.

- Sellers without an eBay store receive fifty free auction listings each month. Final value fees average ten percent of the selling price.

- Sellers with a Basic eBay store pay $15.99 per month. They receive 150 free auction or fixed price listings each month. Final value fees average ten percent of the selling price.

- Sellers with a Premium eBay store pay $59.99 per month. They receive 500 free auction or fixed price listings each month. Final value fees average ten percent of the selling price.

- Sellers with an eBay Anchor store pay $199.99 per month. They receive 2500 free auction or fixed price listings. Final value fees average ten percent of the selling price.

Sellers who subscribe to an eBay store for a one year period can receive additional discounts. Top Rated Sellers who meet certain requirements also qualify for a twenty percent discount on final value fees.

Final Wrap up

Selling on eBay isn't rocket science. Most of it comes down to common sense. Find popular products that people like and enjoy. Offer them at a great price, and treat your customers fairly.

When you're first getting started, sell items you have around the house. It will give you practice listing and monitoring listings. It's also a great way to put a few extra bucks in your pocket, and decide if selling on eBay is right for you.

Pick up your first items to resell at local yard sales, estate sales, and auctions. You can also find some great bargains shopping the clearance aisles at retail stores like Wal-Mart, Target, and T J Maxx. If you live near an outlet mall you should be able to find plenty of items to resell there.

When you list your items keep the six steps to a great listing in mind.

1. **Product research**. Research everything. Look for keywords, description ideas, and pricing info used in listings that closed successfully.

2. **Title**. You have 88 characters to tell the world what you've got. Make every one of them count. Include: maker, model number, color, size, condition, warranty, free shipping, and other relevant info.

3. **Photos**. Use plenty of photos taken from a number of different angles. Make sure your photos are at least 500 pixels on the longest edge, eBay recommends 1600 pixels.

4. **Description**. Keep your description short and to the pint. Use headlines, short sentences, and bullet points. White space is your friend.

5. **Price**. Use the advanced search tool to determine the appropriate starting price for every item you sell. Use a variety of fixed price and auction listings to drive buyers to your other listings or your eBay store.

6. **Shipping / follow up**. Ship your items within the handling period you set, and be sure to include tracking on all items. Use the eBay or PayPal shipping tool to make shipping your items easier. Answer all questions as quickly as possible, and give buyers more info than they asked for.

That's all there is to it.

Good luck and great selling. The **eBay 30 Day Challenge** will help you reach your goals quickly.

www.ingramcontent.com/pod-product-compliance
Lightning Source LLC
Chambersburg PA
CBHW051823170526
45167CB00005B/2137